Cesar Chavez

by Jill C. Wheeler

visit us at
www.abdopub.com

Published by ABDO & Daughters, an imprint of ABDO
Publishing Company, 4940 Viking Drive, Suite 622, Edina,
Minnesota 55435. Copyright ©2003 by Abdo Consulting
Group, Inc. International copyrights reserved in all countries.
No part of this book may be reproduced in any form without
written permission from the publisher.

Printed in the United States.

Edited by Paul Joseph
Graphic Design: John Hamilton
Cover Design: Mighty Media
Interior Photos: AP/Photo, p. 5, 6, 11, 15, 17, 19, 21, 32, 40, 43,
45, 53, 60, 61
Corbis, p. 9, 13, 23, 25, 27, 29, 31, 35, 37, 39, 42, 46, 49, 51, 55,
57, 59

Library of Congress Cataloging-in-Publication Data

Wheeler, Jill C., 1964-
    Cesar Chavez / Jill C. Wheeler.
        p. cm. — (Breaking barriers)
    Includes index.
    Summary: A biography of the Mexican American labor leader
who worked to improve working conditions for migrant farm workers
and to establish the United Farm Workers union.
    ISBN 1-57765-905-8
    1. Chavez, Cesar, 1927- —Juvenile literature. 2. Labor leaders—
United States—Biography—Juvenile literature. 3. United Farm
Workers—Juvenile literature. [1. Chavez, Cesar, 1927- 2. Labor
leaders. 3. Mexican Americans—Biography. 4. United Farm Workers.] I. Title.

HD6509.C48 W484 2003
331.88'13'092—dc21
[B]

2002074668

Contents

Yes, You Can

Eighty-nine-year-old Frank Torres remembers what it was like to be a migrant farm worker. In April 2002, he spoke with a reporter at a community event in Modesto, California. The event celebrated the naming of a local park in honor of labor leader Cesar Chavez.

Chavez spent years toiling in the fields. He only had an eighth-grade education. He never owned a house or a car and never earned more than $6,000 a year. Chavez wanted a better life than this for America's farm workers. He started a movement aimed at better conditions for them. Chavez began America's first successful farm worker's union called the United Farm Workers (UFW).

Torres told the reporter what it had been like before Chavez began the UFW. He talked of how there had been no water for farm workers to drink as they worked in the blazing sun. He remembered how there had been no portable bathrooms in the fields. He recalled the low wages and how he had ached and sweated for only 50 cents an hour. Most of all, he remembered being treated like he didn't matter.

Cesar Chavez

Edward James Olmos, far left wearing a red cap, and actor Martin Sheen, center, march among thousands on April 6, 2002, in Los Angeles, to honor Cesar Chavez and celebrate the 40th anniversary of the United Farm Workers (UFW).

Torres was one of more than 600 people who gathered to remember Cesar Chavez. "He was very gentle-spirited, soft-spoken," said a woman who had worked with Chavez as a volunteer. "Farm workers' living conditions were incredibly poor," she added. "They had no legal right and no rights for collective bargaining. He set about to change that."

Chavez's commitment to better working conditions for farm workers grew to include nonviolent social change and a better environment. Today, Chavez is remembered as more than a crusader for farm workers. He is remembered as a person who empowered people. His motto has become an inspiration for thousands. It is simply, *Si, Se Puede*. Translated, this means, Yes, You Can.

A Farm of His Own

Cesar Estrada Chavez was born on March 31, 1927, near Yuma, Arizona. He was the second of five children born to Librado and Juana Chavez. Young Cesar was named after his grandfather, Cesario Chavez.

Cesario had left Mexico for Arizona Territory in the 1880s. He was one of thousands of settlers to take advantage of the free land there. Those settlers were called homesteaders. Cesario hoped to build a better life for his family on his Arizona homestead. He was proud to own his own farm instead of working on someone else's. Cesario passed down the love of owning his own land to his son Librado.

Librado, in turn, owned his own land. He had a 160-acre (65-ha) farm in Arizona's fertile Gila River Valley. He also owned a small general store and a pool hall. In addition, he worked as the local postmaster. Most days, Librado worked from sunup to sundown. Cesar remembered, "My mom kept the family together."

Cesar Chavez

Cesar's family lived in a large, adobe ranch-style home. Their life was full of hard work, but they were happy. "I had more happy moments as a child then unhappy moments," Cesar recalled.

Cesar sometimes helped his father at the store. Other times, he helped him on the farm. The Chavez family grew vegetables, corn, cotton, and alfalfa. They also raised some livestock. The little farm provided enough food for the family, plus a little extra. Sometimes, they sold the extra food to get money to buy clothes and supplies. Other times, they gave the extra food away to people who didn't have enough to eat.

When Cesar was two years old, the United States's stock market crashed. This started the Great Depression. People across the country lost their jobs and couldn't find new ones. Many people went hungry. Cesar and his siblings had no problem finding people who needed extra food.

In the 1930s, Librado made a business deal with a neighbor to buy more land. But because of the depression, many people did not have any money. They could not pay their bills at the Chavez family's store.

The Chavez family soon found itself in financial trouble. The family owed more than $4,000 in taxes by 1937. And they were unable to pay the debt from the land deal.

Cesar was 10 when the local deputy sheriff came to the family's home. "He had the papers that told us we had to leave, or go to jail," he recalled. For several days, the deputy came every day. Finally, the family had to leave. The state took possession of the farm. The Chavez family could only keep what they could fit in their car.

Unemployed people wait outside the State Labor Bureau in New York City on November 24, 1933, during the Great Depression.

Life as a Migrant

After losing their farm, the Chavez family headed to California. Some people had told them they could find work there that paid well. Librado and Juana were excited. It was hard to find any kind of job during the depression. If they could find good jobs, their children wouldn't have to work.

When the Chavezes arrived in California, they found the situation very different from what they had heard. The work was backbreaking and the wages unbelievably low. At first, the Chavez family worked in the carrot fields. Even when everyone worked a full day, they only earned about two dollars.

Wages were no better in the vineyards or the cotton fields. Sometimes the family worked without being paid at all. They had to scramble to get the money to buy enough gas to drive to the next job. They had no money for a house.

The Chavez family had to live in farm worker camps. The camps were horrible. Workers were crowded into tiny, tar paper shacks with no electricity, bathrooms, or running water. Some workers had to live in their cars. Others camped out under bridges.

Cesar Chavez

Farm workers had to buy supplies from their employers at company stores. The prices at the stores were very high compared to the wages the workers earned. So they often had to buy things on credit. On payday, many workers owed their whole paycheck to the company store. This made it difficult for the workers to get ahead.

Cesar and his brother Richard worked to contribute to the family's income. They shined shoes and sold newspapers. They also collected the foil from empty cigarette packages. Then they sold the foil to get money to buy clothing.

It was hard for the children of farm workers to get an education because they were working to help their families. They constantly moved from one job to the next. As a child, Cesar attended nearly 40 different schools. Many of those schools were segregated. That meant Mexican-Americans were separated from white students. Often, they were teased about their Mexican heritage even though they had been born in America.

Migrant farm workers pull weeds from a field of mustard plants.

In addition, Cesar spoke Spanish at home. The schools demanded all children speak English. "They wouldn't let you talk Spanish," Cesar recalled. "In P.E. they would make you run laps around the track if they caught you speaking Spanish. Or a teacher in a classroom would make you write 'I won't speak Spanish' on the board 300 times… ." Cesar even recalled one teacher who forced Spanish-speaking students to wear a sign that read, "I am a clown, I speak Spanish."

Cesar managed to overcome this adversity and graduate from the eighth grade in 1942. That was the end of his schooling. His father had been hurt in a car accident and couldn't work. Cesar had to leave school for the fields to help the family survive.

Hour after hour, day after day, Cesar worked in the blazing sun. He had to thin lettuce and beets with a short-handled hoe, called *el cortito*. The hoe was so small he had to spend the entire day bent over until his back throbbed in pain. He earned less than 13 cents an hour.

Cesar knew he did not want to spend his life in the fields. He believed there had to be a better way. "I bitterly missed the ranch," he said, "Maybe that is when the rebellion started. Some had been born into the migrant stream. But we had been on the land, and I knew a different way of life. We were poor, but we had liberty. The migrant is poor, and he has no freedom."

These farm workers rose at dawn to thin a lettuce field near Yuma, Arizona.

Navy Blues

Cesar Chavez was used to discrimination. He and his family had been refused service at restaurants and other places because they were Mexican-Americans. He hoped things would be different when he joined the U.S. Navy in 1944.

Seventeen-year-old Chavez wanted to fight for his country. He hoped to be treated like any other soldier. But he quickly learned that even those committed to serving their country experienced discrimination.

Once while on leave, Chavez and some friends went to a movie. Chavez decided to sit in the section marked for whites only. He had paid for his movie ticket and didn't see why he couldn't sit where he wanted. First an usher, then a manager, asked him to leave. He refused. Finally, the theater staff called the police. They pried Chavez's hands off the armrests and hauled him to jail.

At the jailhouse, the police were stumped. They didn't know what crime to charge Chavez with. Chavez hadn't been drunk or disorderly. He hadn't broken any written law. After about an hour, they let him go. It was the first time Chavez had stood up for his rights and took a stand against injustice.

U.S. Navy sailors perch on the USS Missouri on September 2, 1945, for the Japanese surrender ceremony at the end of World War II.

In 1946, Chavez was discharged, and he returned to his family in California. He also returned to the fields. Like other migrant farm workers, he lived by the harvests. Summers meant working in the vineyards. Winters meant working in the cotton fields.

Chavez was not happy to be a farm worker again. However, he was glad to be back home. Several years before, he had met a young woman named Helen Fabela. They had dated before he joined the navy. Now they continued their courtship. On October 22, 1948, they were married in Reno, Nevada. They used some of their meager savings to take a two-week honeymoon trip through California. They returned to make their home in Delano, near San Jose, California.

For the next few years, Chavez bounced between jobs. He wanted to get a job outside of farm work. Yet those jobs were hard to find. And most people didn't want to hire Mexican-Americans. Then he heard that a lumber company in northern California was hiring. He and his brother Richard drove 400 miles (644 km) to see if they could get work there. They were successful, and they worked there for a year and a half. Yet northern California was cool and rainy. Chavez missed San Jose. One day he heard lumber workers were needed there. He jumped at the chance to return.

Cesar Chavez escaped work in the fields by becoming a lumber worker.

Back in San Jose, Chavez had a steady lumber job and a steady paycheck. He and Helen also had three small children, Fernando, Sylvia, and Linda. The family moved to a Mexican-American ghetto called *Sal Si Puedes*. In English, this means Escape if You Can. The Chavez family was one of the fortunate ones in the neighborhood. They had a good home, a loving family, and a steady paycheck. For now, Chavez had escaped the fields. He never forgot that others were not so lucky.

The Power of Change

The Chavez family had always been devoutly Catholic. They believed part of being Catholic was helping others. As a child, Chavez had given extra food away to poor people. As an adult, he worked to convert an old building into a place where Catholics could worship.

Chavez was working alongside the local priest, Father Donald McDonnell. Father McDonnell had come from San Francisco to work with the Mexican-Americans. As Father McDonnell hammered and painted with Chavez, he spoke about the economics of farming. He told Chavez how the Catholic Church felt about workers and justice. McDonnell talked about other people who had fought injustice and won.

Chavez listened carefully. He read books Father McDonnell shared with him. He learned how people like Mohandas Gandhi had used nonviolent protests to enact social change. Chavez started talking with others about changing the lives of migrant workers.

Cesar Chavez

Chavez was not the first to try to make life better for migrant workers. For years, migrant workers had used strikes to protest unfair treatment. When workers strike, they refuse to work until their employer changes things the workers think are unfair.

Chavez's father had participated in strikes. But sometimes employers would not change the practices that the striking workers thought were unfair. The employers would just hire new workers to replace those striking. It seemed there was always someone else willing to do the job. Other times, it was too difficult for the workers to stay on strike for as long as it would take to make their employer address their grievances.

Chavez was thinking about how to change this situation when he met Fred Ross. Ross worked for the Community Service Organization (CSO). He was trying to get Mexican-Americans to unite to improve their lives. He knew he needed a Mexican-American to help him.

Ross had heard good things about Chavez. Several times he went to Chavez's house to talk to him. At first, Chavez refused to see Ross. Chavez didn't trust him. Fred Ross was white. Whites had often treated Chavez and other Mexican-Americans badly. But Ross persisted. Finally, on June 9, 1952, Chavez agreed to talk with him.

Within hours, Chavez agreed to help Ross register Mexican-Americans to vote. "We had never thought that we could actually have any say in our lives," Cesar recalled, "We were poor, we knew it, and we were beyond helping ourselves. Fred Ross opened our eyes—and our minds—to what power we *could* have."

Fred Ross talks with Cesar Chavez at a protest march.

Community Organizer

Within months, Chavez registered more than 2,000 Mexican-Americans to vote. He achieved this by working at it part-time, while performing his regular job during the day. But Chavez's employer thought his organizing activities were interfering with his day job. So Cesar lost his job.

By then, the CSO had realized Chavez's value as a liaison. Mexican-Americans trusted him, and they listened to him. Chavez helped them become U.S. citizens and taught them about their rights as Americans. He taught them about voting. And when they had problems voting, he helped. So when Chavez needed help organizing, the people he had aided repaid the favor.

So the CSO hired Chavez to work for them. He earned $35 a week. It was the most money he had ever earned. Chavez was only in his mid-twenties. Some people thought he was too young for the job. But he knew he could be a good organizer.

Cesar Chavez

Chavez learned by watching how Ross managed a meeting. He paid attention to what made meeting participants respond positively. With the information he gathered, Chavez soon adapted his own style of leading meetings.

Chavez's success at organizing Mexican-Americans frightened some people. They feared Mexican-Americans would become too powerful. They accused Chavez of being a communist.

In spite of this opposition, Chavez continued to work to organize Mexican-Americans. He began to help the CSO register voters outside of San Jose. He moved his family to Madera, California. The CSO increased his salary to $58 a week. The extra money came in handy. Chavez and Helen now had a fourth child, Eloise.

Chavez went to work in Oxnard, California. As he organized workers there, he learned local farm owners were refusing to hire Mexican-Americans to work their fields. Instead, they were bringing in migrant workers from Mexico. These workers were called *braceros*.

*Cesar Chavez leads
a rally to organize
union members.*

Fighting Back

*B*raceros were first used during World War II. The United States and Mexico signed a treaty that said *braceros* could be brought into the U.S. to work the fields since labor was in short supply. However, even after the war when there were plenty of Mexican-Americans to work in the fields, the growers preferred the *braceros*.

The *braceros* were desperate for work. They worked longer hours for less money than Mexican-Americans. They couldn't complain about the horrible working conditions. Nor could they complain about the low pay. Those who did complain lost their job. There were always other *braceros* to take their place.

Day after day, the same thing happened. Field owners and even state officials made it almost impossible for Mexican-Americans to get work in the fields. Chavez knew the field owners were breaking the law so they could pay lower wages and make higher profits.

A migrant worker harvests wine grapes in California.

A Mexican immigrant works in a tomato field.

Chavez worked to organize local Mexican-Americans to call attention to this injustice. He documented how employers were breaking the law. He organized sit-down strikes in the fields. He led marches protesting the lack of jobs for local Mexican-Americans. And he educated journalists about what was happening so they could report on it. Throughout it all, he insisted that people avoid violence. He did not want any part of violent protest.

Chavez and the organized Mexican-Americans were victorious. Growers reluctantly agreed to employ local workers. And some government officials lost their jobs because they had broken laws.

Yet when Chavez returned to Oxnard six months later, the *braceros* were back. Chavez realized there would be no permanent change without a farm workers union. A union could monitor the situation and watch for abuses. Chavez asked the CSO to focus more on organizing farm workers. When the organization refused, he had to make a hard decision. In 1962, he quit.

A Union is Born

Many people did not agree with Chavez's decision to leave the CSO. He had quit a job that paid well. He had a wife and seven children to care for. Paul, Anthony, and Ana had joined the family. And now he was going to try to organize farm workers. But Chavez was committed to helping farm workers have a better life. The family returned to Delano, California. Chavez's wife went to work as a fruit picker so they could earn enough money to feed their children.

Farm workers were not widely organized. Many were afraid of losing their jobs if they tried to organize. They moved around constantly. Plus, farm workers often fought among themselves. The Mexican-American farm workers didn't trust the Filipino farm workers and vice versa. Organizing such a diverse workforce seemed like an impossible goal.

Cesar Chavez

But three years earlier, Chavez's old friend, Father McDonnell, had founded an organization in Stockton, California. It was called the Agricultural Workers Organizing Committee (AWOC). It was affiliated with the American Federation of Labor and Congress of Industrial Organizations (AFL-CIO). A woman named Dolores Huerta had helped Father McDonnell organize the union.

Chavez convinced Huerta to come work for him. He also asked his cousin, Manuel Chavez, to help. Together they started the Farm Workers Association (FWA). Later, it became the National Farm Workers Association (NFWA).

Meanwhile, Chavez worked on recruiting union members around his home in San Jose. There were nearly 90 migrant worker camps in the area. Chavez promised to visit every one of them. Within six months, Chavez had persuaded some 300 workers to join the union. Their dues were $3.50 a month.

Many union members met in Fresno, California, in September 1962. At the meeting, Chavez unveiled a flag to symbolize the union. The red flag featured a white circle with a black eagle in the center.

At the meeting, Chavez spoke of his dreams for the union. He wanted it to be more than a union. He wanted it to be a community dedicated to common goals. He called it *La Causa*, which is Spanish for The Cause. The union motto became *Viva la causa*. That means, Long Live the Cause.

The meeting was a success. Yet members began to leave the union shortly after. At one point, the NFWA had just 12 members paying dues. But Chavez refused to be defeated. He continued to meet with people and talk about *La Causa*. He urged workers to stick together.

In the meantime, he needed to do something big. That opportunity presented itself in 1965 in the vineyards around Delano, California.

Cesar Chavez recruits new members into the NFWA.

Huelga!

Wine grape production is slightly different from that of many other crops. Wine grapes require care year round. In 1965, the people who worked in the vineyards in Delano, California, tended to stay in one place longer than others. The work was hard and low paying. Grape pickers worked in the sun, fought bugs, and dodged chemical spray. For this, they earned about one dollar an hour.

Many of the grape workers were Filipinos. Many also belonged to the AWOC. They were planning a strike to get higher wages. The AWOC leaders asked Chavez if the NFWA members would support their strike. Chavez posed the question to the members. They voted to support the AWOC. They voted for a *huelga*, or strike.

Chavez knew the strike could last a long time. The people who owned the vineyards didn't want to bargain with the workers. Chavez had to find different ways to give the striking workers more power.

A migrant worker harvests grapes in a California field.

Chavez decided to focus the strike on one vineyard at a time. He educated the public about the conditions farm workers faced in the vineyards. He urged people not to buy wines or other products from the targeted vineyard until the owners agreed to bargain with the farm workers.

Cesar Chavez leads a protest urging people to boycott California grapes.

Chavez organized picket lines at the vineyard they chose to target. He asked that all picketers refuse violence, regardless of what happened. This became very hard to do. Representatives of the growers sometimes shot at the striking workers' signs or car windows. The representatives also pushed and shoved the workers. Local law enforcement refused to arrest the growers' representatives.

Chavez organized a 340-mile (547-km) march to call attention to the strike. Marchers walked from Delano to the California state capital in Sacramento. A crowd of 10,000 supporters was waiting to cheer them on when they reached Sacramento.

The first boycott ended in 1966. Workers at the targeted vineyard won a pay raise of 35 cents an hour. The unions then targeted another vineyard, then another. Each time they urged the public not to buy any products produced by the vineyard they were targeting. As the strikes and marches continued, other unions, student groups, and religious groups pledged their support to Chavez and his workers.

As the strike continued, other labor unions, such as the powerful International Brotherhood of Teamsters (IBT), tried to get AWOC and NFWA members to join them instead. The AWOC and NFWA joined forces to become the United Farm Workers Organizing Committee (UFWOC). Later it became the United Farm Workers (UFW).

As the strikes and boycotts dragged on, some of the strikers wanted to use violence. They thought this would bring faster results. But Chavez still believed in nonviolent protest.

In 1968, to show his continued commitment to enacting change by non-violent means, he tried a new tactic to bring attention to *La Causa*. Chavez refused to eat for 25 days. His fast captured the attention of Senator Robert F. Kennedy. Kennedy called Chavez "one of the heroic figures of our time." In addition, Rev. Dr. Martin Luther King, Jr., sent Chavez a telegram of support.

Senator Robert F. Kennedy with Cesar Chavez

Cesar Chavez at a UFW news conference in 1972.

Souring Grapes

In the late 1960s, most wine grape vineyards signed contracts with the UFW. Yet Chavez's work was not done. Workers in vineyards that grew table grapes were also suffering under poor conditions and earning low wages. Chavez urged all Americans to boycott table grapes. The exception to this boycott was table grapes from vineyards with a union contract. To make it easier for buyers to identify these grapes, they were packed in crates marked with the UFW black eagle.

The boycott continued into 1969. May 10 was declared International Grape Boycott Day. British dockworkers refused to unload California grapes. Shipments of California grapes to cities like New York, Chicago, Boston, and Detroit practically stopped. Still the table grape vineyard owners refused to sign union contracts.

Cesar Chavez at a rally in 1970.

Supporters hold a candlelight vigil outside the California governor's mansion in 1970 after Cesar Chavez's imprisonment.

In 1970, Chavez went to Salinas, California, to help with strikes against lettuce growers. He learned that the International Brotherhood of Teamsters had signed contracts with the lettuce growers. The contracts helped the transportation workers but not the field workers. Chavez called for a boycott against a powerful lettuce grower who had signed up with the IBT. The grower obtained a court order to stop the boycott. But Chavez refused to stop it. Chavez was arrested in December 1970. He said, "They can jail us, but they can never jail the Cause."

Chavez's supporters voiced their anger over his imprisonment. The California State Supreme Court heard the case. The justices called for Chavez to be released on Christmas Eve. Four months later, the court determined the lettuce boycott was legal. Chavez immediately urged Americans to stop buying lettuce from non-union growers.

A Lifetime of Work

Throughout the 1970s, Chavez continued to push for reform and justice. He worked constantly to keep the UFW together. In 1970, the UFW moved to new headquarters near Bakersfield, California. The new offices were named *La Paz*, meaning The Peace.

This was not a peaceful time, however. Three UFW members were killed on picket lines in 1972 and 1973. Chavez himself regularly received death threats. He acquired two German shepherd watchdogs to guard the complex. He named them Boycott and *Huelga*.

People began to question Chavez's character. Some people continued to call him a communist. Others said he was power hungry and demanding. They accused him of refusing to let anyone else help lead the UFW. Still other critics said he was arrogant.

Chavez refused to let this criticism interfere with his work. He protested by fasting when necessary. He campaigned and worked with politicians to change laws.

Cesar Chavez

Chavez supported Jerry Brown as governor of California. Brown promoted *La Causa*. Brown won the election and, in 1975, signed the California Agricultural Labor Relations Act. It was the first law that addressed farm worker unions in the United States. The act gave farm workers the right to boycott. It also gave voting rights to migrant seasonal workers.

That same year, a national poll showed that 17 million Americans were honoring the table grape boycott. And perhaps closest to Chavez's heart, the short-handled hoe, *el cortito*, was outlawed.

In 1978, Chavez and the UFW called off the lettuce and table grape boycotts. By then, many growers had signed union contracts. Finally, farm workers around the nation were enjoying better wages, better working conditions, and even health insurance.

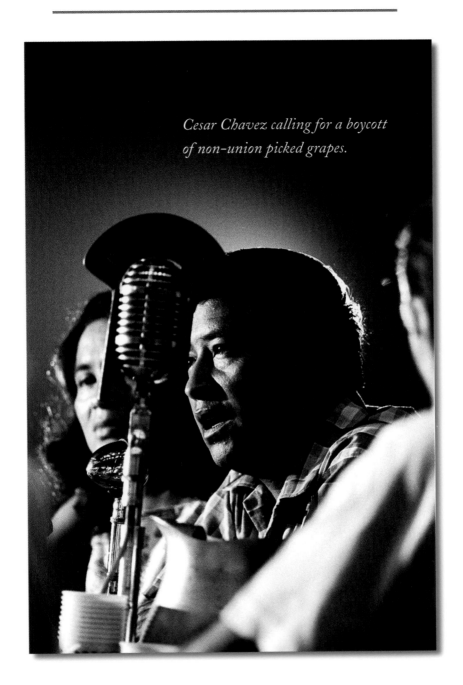

Cesar Chavez calling for a boycott of non-union picked grapes.

An Invisible Enemy

In the 1980s, Chavez turned his attention to pesticides. Growers routinely used hundreds of pesticides to keep their crops free of bugs, disease, and weeds. Chavez was concerned about the effects of pesticides on farm workers. In the 1960s, farm workers had begun to show symptoms of pesticide poisoning. The UFW had been investigating the issue over the years since.

In 1984, Chavez urged Americans to boycott grapes again. This time, it was because of pesticide residue on grapes. The UFW produced a movie about the dangers of pesticides in 1987. The movie showed how farm workers suffered from unusually high rates of birth defects and cancer. Chavez traveled around the country showing the movie. He used it to raise awareness of the dangers of pesticides. In 1988, he went on a 36-day fast to protest pesticide use. Soon, celebrities and activists joined the crusade.

A crop duster sprays
pesticide over a field.

Meanwhile, the UFW was suffering. The mood in California had become more pro-business. Powerful multinational corporations were taking over many small farms. These giant organizations did not want to bargain with farm workers. Even the California Agricultural Labor Relations Board was more likely to rule in favor of growers than of workers. The UFW began to win fewer contracts. And fewer UFW-supported candidates won elections.

Chavez refused to let these setbacks stop him. He and other UFW workers organized strikes to protest the lack of drinking water and bathrooms in some fields. Chavez also led about 10,000 supporters in a protest march in the Salinas Valley. The marchers sought better working conditions.

In 1991, the government of Mexico awarded Chavez the Aztec Eagle Award. The award honors people of Mexican heritage who have made major contributions outside of Mexico.

Cesar Chavez urges the public not to buy grapes that have been sprayed with pesticide.

A Fight to the Finish

In April 1993, Chavez traveled to Arizona. A large lettuce grower had sued the UFW for damages incurred during a boycott. The grower filed the lawsuit in Arizona. Lawyers for the grower thought the Arizona courts might favor them over the farm workers. Chavez arrived to help defend the UFW in the court case.

On the evening of April 22, Chavez and other UFW staffers stayed at the home of a friend. Chavez was exhausted from two days of grueling testimony. He went to bed early. Chavez died in his sleep that night.

Chavez was only 66 years old. Years of field labor, protest fasts, and endless work had taken their toll on his body. Some believed he had never really regained his strength after his last fast in 1988.

Chavez's funeral was held on April 29, 1993. It was the largest funeral of any labor leader in history. More than 20,000 mourners attended, including farm workers from as far away as Florida. Chavez was buried at the *La Paz* complex, in front of his office.

Cesar Chavez

On August 8, 1994, Helen Chavez traveled to the White House. She was there to accept the Medal of Freedom for her husband from President Bill Clinton. The Medal of Freedom is the highest honor a civilian can receive. In the award presentation, President Clinton praised Chavez for having "faced formidable, often violent opposition with dignity and nonviolence."

Before his death, Chavez had worried about the future of the UFW. He had struggled constantly to maintain the union. Even during his lifetime, membership had dropped from a high of more than 30,000 to just 12,000.

Chavez's son-in-law, Arturo Rodriguez, succeeded Chavez as president of the UFW. Together with Dolores Huerta, he began to rebuild UFW membership and keep Chavez's vision alive.

In 2000, Californians voted for Senate Bill 984. This bill created the Cesar Chavez Day of Service and Learning. Cesar Chavez's birthday, March 31, is now a holiday in California. This day celebrates the accomplishments of a man who dedicated his life to improving the lives of others.

Cesar Chavez

Timeline

March 31, 1927: Cesar Estrada Chavez is born on a farm near Yuma, Arizona.

1942: Chavez helps support his family by dropping out of school and working in the fields.

1944: Chavez joins the U.S. Navy.

1952: Chavez is recruited by Fred Ross into the Community Service Organization (CSO).

1952-1962: Chavez helps organize 22 CSO chapters.

1962: The first convention of the National Farm Workers Association (NFWA) is held.

1965: Chavez begins a strike against grape growers. Millions rally to the cause.

1970: Chavez is jailed after refusing to stop a boycott against lettuce growers.

1984: Chavez begins a protest against pesticides that make farm laborers sick.

April 22, 1993: Cesar Chavez dies.

1994: Chavez is posthumously awarded the Medal of Freedom by President Clinton.

Web Sites

Would you like to learn more about Cesar Chavez?
Please visit **www.abdopub.com** to find up-to-date
Web site links about Cesar Chavez and the United
Farm Workers (UFW). These links are routinely
monitored and updated to provide the most current
information available.

*Cesar Chavez talks to the media
during a farm labor protest rally.*

Glossary

AFL-CIO

Stands for the American Federation of Labor and Congress of Industrial Organizations. The AFL-CIO is an organization of trade unions in the United States.

boycott

To refrain from having any dealings with something, such as to refuse to buy anything produced by a particular company.

civilian

A person who is not a police officer, a firefighter, or in the military.

collective bargaining

Negotiations between employers and employees about terms and conditions of employment. Employees usually are represented by a union in collective bargaining.

communist

A person who believes in the concept or system of society in which the major resources and means of production are owned by the community rather than by individuals.

discrimination

To treat some people differently from others because of their race, religion, gender, or some other factor.

Great Depression

The worst and longest economic collapse in the history of the industrial world.

International Brotherhood of Teamsters (IBT)

A union representing workers in transportation and other fields.

Mohandas Gandhi

An Indian lawyer and political activist who worked to gain India its independence from Great Britain.

pesticides

Chemicals used to kill bugs, treat plant diseases, or kill weeds in crops.

residues

Chemicals from pesticides that are left over on plants grown for crops.

segregation

When races are kept separate from one another.

Index